Chosen

A Devotional for the Modern Woman Who Has Loved, Lost and Found a Path Forward

Dr. Mia McNeil

BEVERLY
HOUSE

BEVERLY HOUSE PRESS

Internal Design, and Illustrations © 2024 by Beverly House Press, LLC
The cover title for this book was set in Born Ready Slanted licensed by Nicky Laatz The cover text for this book was set in Questral font.

Published by Beverly House Press
304 E. Pine St. #1058
Lakeland, FL 33801
www.BeverlyHousePress.com

Library of Congress Control Number: 2024908151

ISBN: 978-1-957466-08-8 (Hardback)
ISBN: 978-1-957466-09-5 (Paperback)
ISBN: 978-1-957466-20-0 (ePub)

Dedicated in the memory of my late husband Mack.
Thank you for choosing me to journey alongside you until the end of
our love story.

Contents

Foreword

To the woman who is reading this: the one who loves deeply, the one who feels lost, or the one who is crying out in the midst of finding her footing to move forward, I pray that this devotional, written by my close and trusted friend, will help you overcome by the blood of the Lamb and by the powerful word of her testimony (Revelation 12:11).

Mia has a lot of titles: Mom. Doctor. Daughter. Sister. Friend. Nana. Minister... But there's one particular title she never could have imagined being: Widow.

Mia's testimony echoes God's faithfulness through the gripping depths of grief. Her words are born from tears shed in agony. In her despair, she turned to Jesus and leaned on the promises of God to guide her through the darkest of days. In pain, she found strength. In sorrow, she found hope. And in tears, she found solace in the arms of a loving and merciful God.

I met Mia in 2019 in a beautiful church in Easton, Pennsylvania. The timing was a divinely ordained kind of timing by God. He knew we needed each other in that particular season of life. As she was learning to navigate a new season of grief while carrying deep pain, incredible sadness, and a new life where nothing was the same, I was learning to navigate a new season of salvation, being recently saved by Christ, carrying deep joy, incredible excitement, and a new life where nothing was the same.

Mia was at the very bottom of her muddy and dark wilderness, and I was at the top of my immaculate and bright mountaintop when our lives intersected. But because Mia was deeply rooted in Christ, even in her grief, she locked arms with me and taught me how to hear the voice of God, discipled me in prayer and intercession, and was an incredible friend who truly mirrored how to love like our Lord and Savior. She challenged me and she taught me the truth – even in her darkest of days.

Here we are now, Mia shouting from her mountaintop with a roar like a lion, forged in fire, sharpened by pain, arms lifted in victory, and testifying of the God who heals, redeems, and restores.

There's a transformative power that comes from community and from writing out the pain. I pray that this devotional leads you to soak in the presence of God. He is with you: Just like He was with Mia. Just like He was with Ruth. It's time for your heart to heal. It's time to walk in His holy power. It's time to navigate the path forward.

You are Chosen for such a time as this.

With love,

Tracy Onyekanne, Emmy Award Winning Host

Introduction

It was March 25, 2019. I vividly remember sitting in my room in the quiet of the night with a feeling of numbness and disbelief. My 18-year-old daughter laid in my arms, unable to fall asleep, while the other three slept peacefully spread throughout the immaculately curated master bedroom. We had just moved into our new house six months prior. So how could it be that God would choose to take my husband and partner of nearly 17 years now?

It did not make sense for him to be taken now that we were finally living the life we had dreamed of. Yet, on that day, he took his last breath on this side of heaven, while I stayed here, about to face the darkest season of my life.

Our four girls still needed their father, and I still needed my best friend, but God had a different plan.

Four days later, we drove up to the church where two large American flags were floating in the calm wind firmly attached to the ladders of two local fire trucks. On that day, I remember shaking hands of uniformed civil servants, from police and fire-fighters to military members, more than one could count. Family and friends came from near and far to offer kind words, meals and support, but eventually, they all returned to their lives as I mustered the strength to face my own.

In the following months, the house felt cold and empty. By then, Spring had sprung and new life was evident through the many windows of our beautiful house. Unfortunately, the weight of my new reality weighed too heavily for me to care. There was no more joy, no more laughter, no more home-cooked meals – just lots of hugs, quiet tears and takeout food.

Overnight, I became responsible for paying all the bills and cooking our meals, a responsibility my South Carolinian late husband had gladly taken on from the time we dated; we used to eat good y'all! Needless to say, I had planned a very different life for myself and my family, and this was far from it.

Of all people, I never thought I would be writing a devotional on the book of Ruth. Growing up in church, I heard various interpretations of this book but never grasped the depth of the life-giving message and destiny-shaping this book holds. The life of a young widow gleaning in the field and marrying an older rich man was not relatable to me.

Her story seemed overhyped and did not resonate at all. In hindsight, and in all honesty, I understand now that I was closed off to receiving the gems sprinkled throughout the story, because my heart was misaligned with God's way of doing things. I could not relate, because I did not want to relate. My heart was not willing to submit to the will of God the way Ruth had surrendered.

Ironically, all these years later, here I am, a widow, gleaning in the fields of my new life just like Ruth. God has chosen this story to shape my understanding of destiny and purpose and also opened my heart to restoration and to accepting his ultimate plan for my life.

I never realized how much life and purpose could be found after a season of devastating loss until rediscovering the story of Ruth. Life after any type of loss is hard, but the power of faith and the role of community are undeniably important to the healing process. Ruth's life journey brought me hope in the midst of my own healing journey, and I am deeply convinced that the same will be true for you.

You may have navigated many difficult life experiences on your own, but this time, you won't have to do it alone. This devotional is filled with universal life themes and lessons that can be applied to the life of any woman in pursuit of healing and purpose beyond life's most painful experiences.

If you have felt discouraged, hopeless and heartbroken, I believe that you will find comfort and hope in this book. Whether you have lost a loved one, ended a marriage or experienced any such adversity that has hurt you to your core, this book will help you find yourself again.

This devotional contrasts the story of Ruth with my own. One story is staged in biblical times, while the other tells the upheavals of a woman living in this modern world. This devotional presents you with a unique opportunity to see your life's challenges through a lens of hope. The full story of Ruth will be told through my own lens while staying true to the Scriptures. You will then enter my world and navigate through my journey of love, loss and healing.

Read on as I share a biblical and modern perspective on the beauty and purpose found beyond deep emotional pain – a reality which is accessible to us all through faith as defined in the message version of Hebrews 11:1, "The fundamental fact of existence is that this trust in God, this faith, is the firm foundation under everything that makes life worth living. It's our handle on what we cannot see."

If you are in need of more support, download the Navigating Grief Survival Guide:
https://www.McneilPsychiatric.com/free-grief-guide
and reach out to me or one of the professionals at Hello Healing Network.

How to Use This Book:

The book is divided into five sections. Each section includes three entries focused on the story of Ruth followed by three entries focused on my story.

Here are a few guiding steps to get the most out of this devotional journal:

1 - Pray that God would reveal himself

2 - Read the Bible passage

3 - Read the daily devotion

4 - Meditate on the word of God

5 - Write a personal/practical application or journal entry (see prompts)

6 - Close in prayer

Each entry depicting Ruth's story will include a reading from the book of Ruth and a prayer. You will then enter my world and get to walk through my own journey of love, loss and healing and be invited to journal with the guidance of journaling prompts.

By the end of this devotional, you will have read the entire book of Ruth, and hopefully, you feel motivated to keep going!

Part I: The Last Goodbye

Death Is Not the End

*Both Mahlon and Kilion also died, and Naomi
was left without her two sons and her husband.*

Ruth 1:5

In the first chapter of the book of Ruth, we are introduced to
Elimelech, his wife Naomi and their sons Malhon and Kilion.
We learn about a famine in Bethlehem and of the family's move
to the country of Moab. In a span of ten years, Naomi, the dutiful
wife and mother, has buried her husband and her two sons, losing
both her providers and her protectors.

Without family, support, providers or protectors in a foreign
land, Naomi found herself in an impossible situation with a difficult choice to make. She could stay in Moab among pagan people
alongside her native daughters-in-law, also now young widows, or

go home to Bethlehem where God had visited His people and given them food after the famine.

Amid the devastating loss of her husband and two sons, God had a plan that even death and sorrow could not cancel. God needed Naomi and Ruth for a greater purpose that would only be revealed in time. The many tears they shed could not be compared to the destiny that awaited them – a destiny connected to the Savior of the world himself, Jesus Christ. The apostle Paul said it this way: "For I consider that the sufferings of this present time are not worth comparing with the glory that is to be revealed in us" (Romans 8:18).

When we lose a loved one, it can seem like death is the end, which is not entirely false. Indeed, death closes the door to a season of one's life, but it is not the end of everything. Mourning and grieving are necessary steps to the healing process, but above all, we have a responsibility to respond to God favorably when He calls us out of that season to fulfill His predestined plan.

In my own personal journey, I found myself curious about my purpose after becoming a widow left to raise four children.

"What good could come out of this?" I asked myself.

"How could a good God allow such heartbreak?"

When our plans, dreams and hopes are abruptly canceled by life's unpredictability, we have a choice to make. It is for us to look for the meaning of the loss. It is a process which requires time, courage and an open heart. Whatever has been lost is gone, but more life awaits you if you are willing to go on. No one can understand the pain of losing a husband like a wife, but beyond the loss, more life awaits. Naomi and Ruth dared to believe that death was not the end, and God showed Himself faithful.

Reading: Ruth 1:1-5

1 In the days when the judges ruled, there was a famine in the land. So a man from Bethlehem in Judah, together with his wife and two sons, went to live for a while in the country of Moab.

2 The man's name was Elimelek, his wife's name was Naomi, and the names of his two sons were Mahlon and Kilion. They were Ephrathites from Bethlehem, Judah. And they went to Moab and lived there.

3 Now Elimelek, Naomi's husband, died, and she was left with her two sons.

4 They married Moabite women, one named Orpah and

the other Ruth. After they had lived there about ten years,

5 both Mahlon and Kilion also died, and Naomi was left without her two sons and her husband.

Pray with me

Dear God, the weight I am carrying today is too heavy for me to bear on my own. I pray that Your strength is made perfect in my weakness. Keep me close to You so that I may experience Your presence; increase my faith, so I can believe beyond what I see. In Thy name, Amen.

Purpose Partners

Where you go I will go, and where you stay I will stay. Your people will be my people and your God my God.

Ruth 1:16b

We cannot afford to be at the wrong place at the wrong time if we are going to live purposefully. Giving room for the Holy Spirit to lead us and guide us in discerning the beginning and ending of a season is key if we are going to fulfill our God-given purpose.

Naomi was a sojourner in Moab, and after spending ten years away from home, it was finally time to return to Bethlehem. God had a plan prepared before the foundation of the world that could only be set in motion after the death of Elimelech, Chilion and Mahlon. The ending of their life in Moab was connected to the coming of Jesus Christ – literally! Ruth was destined to be the carrier of a blessed seed, and Naomi was her assigned purpose partner.

To carry out God's plan, Naomi and Ruth would need to partner up. While Naomi wished to return to Bethlehem alone, God had placed in Ruth a strong desire to follow Naomi to Bethlehem. Ruth had enough faith to believe in the God of Israel and reject the pagan gods of her own people (Ruth 1:16).

We must be intentional about those we allow to lead us, and who we choose to follow.

Being a widow in a foreign land, Naomi's chances of survival were rather bleak. Her social status had changed, and while Ruth could've returned to her father's house, and been provided for, she showed great faith and courage by following Naomi. Sometimes, we must make a bold move to reach our next level in life, and that includes setting boundaries in our relationships, because not everyone is meant to join us in our next season.

Orpah remained in Moab, because she was not assigned to Naomi and Ruth's next season. Purpose partners are value-aligned, committed and faithful. They are not self-serving, but rather, they are willing and wanting to serve. Purpose partners help facilitate the destiny plan God has for us. The relationship is easy, and the connection is not forced. Just like Ruth was committed to Naomi's well-being, your purpose partner wants to see you win at all cost. Their intentions are clear, and their words match their actions.

There is no shame in saying goodbye when a season ends. It takes a lot of wisdom and self-control to let go, even when the love is still there. Asking God for discernment and confirmation is a necessary step to align with those God has assigned in our life.

Reading: Ruth 1:6-18

6 When Naomi heard in Moab that the Lord had come to the aid of his people by providing food for them, she and her daughters-in-law prepared to return home from there.

7 With her two daughters-in-law she left the place where she had been living and set out on the road that would take them back to the land of Judah.

8 Then Naomi said to her two daughters-in-law, "Go back, each of you, to your mother's home. May the Lord show you kindness, as you have shown kindness to your dead husbands and to me.

9 May the Lord grant that each of you will find rest in the home of another husband."Then she kissed them goodbye and they wept aloud

10 and said to her, "We will go back with you to your people."

11 But Naomi said, "Return home, my daughters. Why would you come with me? Am I going to have any more sons, who could become your husbands?

12 Return home, my daughters; I am too old to have another husband. Even if I thought there was still hope for me—even if I had a husband tonight and then gave birth to sons—

13 would you wait until they grew up? Would you remain unmarried for them? No, my daughters. It is more bitter for me than for you, because the Lord's hand has turned against me!"

14 *At this they wept aloud again. Then Orpah kissed her mother-in-law goodbye, but Ruth clung to her.*

15 *"Look," said Naomi, "your sister-in-law is going back to her people and her gods. Go back with her.*

16 *But Ruth replied, "Don't urge me to leave you or to turn back from you. Where you go I will go, and where you stay I will stay. Your people will be my people and your God my God.*

17 *Where you die I will die, and there I will be buried. May the Lord deal with me, be it ever so severely, if even death separates you and me."*

18 When Naomi realized that Ruth was determined to go with her, she stopped urging her.

Pray with me

Dear God, in this season of my life, I desire to be surrounded by the people you have assigned to my purpose. I pray for discernment to know the people to welcome in my life and the courage to let some people go. I am willing to go where You send me and do what You would have me do. In Thy name, Amen.

Thank God for the Barley Season

So Naomi returned from Moab accompanied by Ruth the Moabite, her daughter-in-law, arriving in Bethlehem as the barley harvest was beginning.

Ruth 1:22

The Scriptures teach us that for everything there is a season and a time for every matter under heaven (Ecclesiastes 3). At times, it may appear that some people have more grief and sorrow than others. But in reality, we all have our share of burdens to face and difficulties to overcome. Thankfully, just like in nature, every season of life has a beginning and an ending.

Naomi and Ruth arrived in Bethlehem at the beginning of the barley season which would last 40 to 55 days. Ruth decided to venture out and glean behind the harvesters in hopes of finding favor among the reapers and picking up the grain leftover for the poor.

According to Ruth 2:3b, "She happened to come to the part of the field belonging to Boaz," who was of the clan of Elimelech. Interestingly enough, Naomi did not ask Boaz for help although he was a close relative. We do not know her reason for not reaching out to him, but it would be fair to speculate that she could have been dissuaded by feelings of shame or pride. Regardless of her motive, God had a plan.

Indeed, Ruth gleaning in Boaz' field was far from a coincidence and was in fact in God's divine plan. Over the following weeks, her character and hard work would attract favor both from men and from God. And while it seems like nothing exciting was happening in her life, a major breakthrough was coming. God, who is in control of the times and circumstances of our lives, was orchestrating a beautiful end to this dry season in Ruth's life.

Ruth worked until the end of the barley and wheat harvest. It was then that Naomi said to her, "My daughter, should I not seek rest for you so that it may be well with you?"

Ruth left her country, her people, and the security of her community only to find herself a poor widow spending long days gleaning in a field far away from home. She did not become bitter or resentful but rather gracefully endured this humbling season of her life. She trusted God who, at a moment's notice, would change the course of her story. His plan of restoration would be perfect and complete. She would finally enter a season of rest, which is God's desire for all of his children.

Ruth 1:19-22

19 *So the two women went on until they came to Bethlehem. When they arrived in Bethlehem, the whole town was stirred because of them, and the women exclaimed, "Can this be Naomi?"*

20 *"Don't call me Naomi," she told them. "Call me Mara, because the Almighty has made my life very bitter.*

21 *I went away full, but the Lord has brought me back empty. Why call me Naomi? The Lord has afflicted me; the Almighty has brought misfortune upon me."*

22 *So Naomi returned from Moab accompanied by Ruth the Moabite, her daugh-*

ter-in-law, arriving in Bethle-
hem as the barley harvest was
beginning.

Pray with me

Dear God, I honor You for being a consistent provider. When I look back over my life, I see how You have always been there for me. Today, I humbly put my unwavering faith in Your hands and trust in You for a better tomorrow. In Thy name, Amen.

The Saddest Spring Ever

Even when I walk through the darkest valley, I will not be afraid, for you are close beside me.

Psalm 23:4

D eath came knocking at my door on a cold early Spring morning.

I woke up to words that haunt me to this day.

"Mommy, Mommy," my 11-year-old screamed as she rushed into my bedroom.

"I think Daddy's dead!"

Overnight, my life changed without warning. I was no longer a suburban wife. It was just hours before that my late husband and I were laying in bed, talking about the upcoming week, when the rising heat in the room caught him by surprise. He liked to keep the room cool, but we were long past the days where we bickered about the room temperature. So when I admitted to adjusting the thermostat to warm up our freezing room, he simply said, "Babe, it's okay. I'll sleep on the couch." These were his last words to me. It was the last time I would see him alive.

Just a few days later, I would walk with my four daughters behind a light blue casket, say my goodbyes, and bury a life that was no longer mine. Death stole the future we had carefully planned. Death stole the dreams we dreamed together, and for a moment, death had me question the sovereign will of God. It was only then that the notion of death became real to me.

Hearing about death and experiencing it are very distinct realities. For me, this abrupt separation without the chance to say goodbye was like detaching a part from my body without anesthesia. It felt cruel. It was a mind-numbing, devastating pain like nothing I had ever experienced before. No one prepared me for this, and while I wanted to wake up from this nightmare, I could not escape it. I was aloof to the long road to healing that was ahead of me, and so, death and I sat in the same room for months, but no healing could take place because I was frozen in time; I was stuck.

Over time, we would become very well acquainted. Death would teach me things I did not know about myself, and it would teach me a side of God that was only accessible to me through this painful reality. My faith was shaken. I asked God many questions, and many of them remained without an answer. I found myself angry with God and wrestled with the timing of my very best friend slipping away. I was not ready but have since made peace with God's will.

Death was not the end. It was instead the beginning of a new life. A life I did not ask for, pray for or ever imagined, but it was mine to figure out, and I did. "Until death do us part" was our vow. His death was never meant to be the end of my life. I know this now.

Pray with me

Dear God, goodbyes hurt and while I have more tears than words today, I also have my belief in a God who restores broken hearts. In Thy name, Amen.

Key themes: grief, loss, parenting, starting over

Guided Journaling:

1. Look at the key themes listed above. What key theme(s) resonate with you and why?

2. Can you think of a significant loss that challenged your faith in God?

3. In hindsight, what did you learn about God from that situation?

When Community Gets Complicated

Do not be afraid or discouraged, for the Lord will personally go ahead of you. He will be with you; he will neither fail you nor abandon you.

Deuteronomy 31:8

After my husband's untimely passing, I was surrounded by family and friends for the first few weeks. Meals, fruit baskets, cards, plants and comforting words were pouring in. God provided many angels to help us through the initial shock and early grief stages.

There are times when I've felt terribly alone even while being well-surrounded. I can remember wanting to be alone and having so many people around me and other times wishing that one per-son would ring my doorbell or call my phone.

However, when I look back at it now, I can count on, one hand, the people God assigned to be part of that phase in my journey.

My feelings were hurt by some individuals whom I considered to be close friends but surprisingly did not show up as I expected – people who gained access to my home and to my heart, with perhaps not enough discernment on my part.

I can also think of a few individuals who were most certainly assigned to that season of my life but were never meant to partner with me for the long haul. I made peace with it all, no longer confusing an assignment for attachment. I learned many years ago that some friends are for a reason, some friends are for a season and only a few are for a lifetime.

In my darkest times, I did not need a crowd. I did not need a tribe. I needed God Himself and the individuals God assigned to each season of grief and healing. At some point, it was my mother, then my sister, my spiritual mother/aunt, cousins, girlfriends, col-leagues and many times God used my own children.

Ultimately, after letting misaligned and temporary friendships run their course, I wrote a prayer to God asking for the friends and purpose partners assigned to my life and my calling. He an-swered me, and I have seen how He cares about every aspect of my life through a community of God-fearing women He has placed around me. I have learned to not take people for granted but instead value their role in my life. Many have touched my life for the better, whether for a reason, a season or until now, and for this, I am deeply grateful.

Pray with me

Dear God, thank you for the friendships that provided gentle comfort and for the ones that taught me hard lessons. I pray that I too, can be a friend that sticks closer than a brother, just as Jesus has been to me. In Thy name, Amen.

Key themes: family, friends, support, forgiveness

Guided Journaling:

1. Look at the key themes listed above. What key theme(s) resonate with you and why?

2. Did your community show up for you when you were going through difficult times? How did that make you feel?

3. What are some benefits of having support and community around you and your family?

4. List the names of individuals you would like to include in your support system and commit to reaching out when needed.

A Humbling Season

God is our refuge and strength, an ever-present help in trouble.

Psalm 46:1

I vividly remember sitting in front of my MacBook screen and being blindsided by yet another change. No one prepared me for the fact that I could no longer check off the "married" box on any official document and that I had to own up to my new status of being a "widow." This was such a contrast to the joy of going from "single" to "married." And as simple as this task appeared to be, I was simply not ready.

That day, I cried and I sobbed. I was not ready to be widowed; I certainly was not ready to be a family of five. I did not want to be excluded from activities for couples. I did not want to parent four teenage girls alone. It seemed all too new and too cruel. Being widowed would force me into a humbling season that challenged my social standing, my family constellation and even my financial status.

God often uses adversity to deepen our faith and develop our godly character, but at that point, I would've gladly bypassed having to grieve and grow in my faith simultaneously. And so, with every milestone of my healing journey, I leaned more and more into God and the Scripture.

I found support from my community, but this could not compare to the comfort and peace I found in trusting God with the details of my new life. Truth is, I could not afford to do life on my own because I had so much to lose. My children, my career, and my literal mind were all at stake. So I carried this heavy cross as gracefully as I could but never without God.

In that season, I prayed humble prayers. I did not know how to parent four young ladies by myself, how to make the right decision about housing and schools, and how to ensure their mental, emotional, physical and moral safety while modeling a faith worth contending for. Ultimately, I firmly believed that God would take care of us and He did. In time, most aspects of my life flourished, and I can testify that we never lacked anything. All the glory belongs to God.

Pray with me

Dear God, may I abide in you and you in me whenever life gets difficult and I struggle to find my way. In Thy name, Amen.

Key themes: social status, humility, faith

Guided Journaling:

1. Look at the key themes listed above. What key theme(s) resonate with you and why?

2. Describe a humbling season that deepened your faith and relationship with God?

3. List areas of your life that cause you to operate in pride and present an opportunity for repentance?

Part 2: Survival

Imitate the Faith

And Ruth the Moabite said to Naomi, "Let me go to the field and glean among the ears of grain after him in whose sight I shall find favor." And she said to her, "Go, my daughter."

Ruth 2:2

Naomi had all the reasons in the world to be bitter after suffering such heavy losses. In her own words, "I went away full and the Lord has brought me back empty" (Ruth 1:21).

Death was all around her and hope had faded away.

However, she failed to realize that she had not come back home "empty." She actually came back with everything she needed for where God was taking her. In her case, it was Ruth, her daughter-in-law. What we think we need is not always in God's plan for where God is taking us. In this instance, the two women would need a whole lot of faith, and they would need each other. Ruth's faith was rooted in Naomi's own walk with God.

Ruth watched Naomi bury a husband and two sons. She observed her process after losing her security, her protectors and providers. As a new convert, Ruth started as a witness of faith and eventually became an imitator of Naomi's faith. As it is written in Hebrews 6:11-12, "And we desire that each one of you show the same diligence to the full assurance of hope until the end, that you do not become sluggish, but imitate those who through faith and patience inherit the promises." Ruth became an imitator of Naomi, whose faith would stand as a building block for Ruth's own relationship with the God of Israel. God trusted Naomi with hardship. She had the capacity to be used by God even with a broken heart.

What about you and me? Ask yourself, "Can God trust me with a broken heart?"

Have you ever wondered whether your own trials were connected to someone else's destiny? The way in which we suffer when walking though painful situations determines whether God can use us to support others, and imitating the faith of Naomi and Ruth is a good place to start. Even when life blindsides us with painful experiences, it is God's plan that must ultimately prevail. We are here to serve a higher purpose, and we are therefore called to build our faith and live by faith.

Ruth 2:1-7

1 Now Naomi had a relative of her husband's, a worthy man of the clan of Elimelech, whose name was Boaz.

2 And Ruth the Moabite said to Naomi, "Let me go to the field and glean among the ears of grain after him in whose sight I shall find favor." And she said to her, "Go, my daughter."

3 So she set out and went and gleaned in the field after the reapers, and she happened to come to the part of the field belonging to Boaz, who was of the clan of Elimelech.

4 And behold, Boaz came from Bethlehem. And he said to the reapers, "The Lord be with you!" And they answered, "The Lord bless you."

5 Then Boaz said to his young man who was in charge of the reapers, "Whose young woman is this?"

6 And the servant who was in charge of the reapers answered, "She is the young Moabite woman, who came back with Naomi from the country of Moab.

7 She said, 'Please let me glean and gather among the sheaves after the reapers.' So she came, and she has continued from early morning until now, except for a short rest.

Pray with me

Dear God, build my faith when my heart is troubled. Teach me to lean into You and trust You whatever life brings my way. In Thy name, Amen.

Favored Beyond Broken

*The Lord repay you for what you have done,
and a full reward be given you by the Lord, the
God of Israel, under whose wings you have come
to take refuge!*

Ruth 2:12

Our brokenness, limitations and setbacks are the ideal platform for God to be God. While Ruth and Naomi had limited resources, their set of circumstances hid limitless potential.

Naomi carried deep wisdom and life experience, while Ruth was humble and obedient (Ruth 3:5-6). Together, they applied a virtuous code of conduct and modeled how to walk through adversity gracefully.

"Only good things were said of Ruth" who rapidly gained a good reputation among the Jews. The word was out and it was in her favor. Even Boaz heard about the way Ruth treated Naomi, and it was common knowledge that she was of good moral character.

Truth be told, you never know who is watching. Even when you're going through difficult times, the world does not stop watching. In fact, we are at times subject to more scrutiny because, as women of faith, we are held to a higher standard. Managing high emotions after suffering from a broken heart is no easy task, but it is possible. Ruth did not allow her circumstances to taint her character, which surely attracted God's favor.

While the Bible is not very descriptive about Ruth and Naomi's healing journey, we can assume that they had a lot of emotional trauma to process and heal from. They suffered together and healed as a family. They took refuge at home where God provided healing and blessings. God provided for all of their needs, and He wants to do the very same for you.

As the Apostle Peter wrote: "After you have suffered a little while, the God of all grace, who has called you to his eternal glory in Christ, will himself restore, confirm, strengthen and establish you" (1 Peter 5:10).

There is a safety found in God the Father if we would look to Him when our hearts are afflicted and when we face despair. There is refuge under His wings where we can find safety while we heal and hope for better days.

Ruth 2:8-13

8a Then Boaz said to Ruth,
"Now, listen, my daughter, do

not go to glean in another field or leave this one, but keep close to my young women.

9 Let your eyes be on the field that they are reaping, and go after them. Have I not charged the young men not to touch you? And when you are thirsty, go to the vessels and drink what the young men have drawn."

10 Then she fell on her face, bowing to the ground, and said to him, "Why have I found favor in your eyes, that you should take notice of me, since I am a foreigner?"

11 But Boaz answered her, "All that you have done for your mother-in-law since the death of your husband has been fully told to me, and how you left your father and mother and your native land and came to a people that you did not know before.

12 The Lord repay you for what you have done, and a full reward be given you by the Lord, the God of Israel, under whose wings you have come to take refuge!"

13 Then she said, "I have found favor in your eyes, my lord, for you have comforted me and spoken kindly to your servant, though I am not one of your servants."

Pray with me

Dear God, I look to you for restoration and healing. I give You permission to heal my heart and give me a fresh perspective on what has been lost and where You are taking me. In Thy name, Amen.

Arranged Marriage

"Blessed be the man who took notice of you." So she told her mother-in-law with whom she had worked and said, "The man's name with whom I worked today is Boaz."

Ruth 2:19b

How would you feel about an arranged marriage? Who would you trust to counsel you through that process?

Marriage is no small commitment; it goes way beyond the actual nuptials. In our modern world, this decision is often influenced by culture, parents, past relationships and even religious beliefs. In Ruth's days, there were very clear rules about marriage and specifically one ending in the death of a husband. Naomi was very conscious of Ruth's limited options and had her best interest at heart.

God sends wise counselors our way to help us navigate the ups and downs of life. Oftentimes, the challenge is in how we discern those who are meant to help us and how we receive wise counsel.

Ruth is a good example of humility and wisdom. She listened to Naomi's discerning voice and followed instruction, never suspecting that her obedience would lead her to marry into Abraham's bloodline. Ruth was a convert and displayed great faith. It was not about how long she served Yahweh but rather how she walked out her faith. Ruth's marriage to Boaz was in fact an arranged marriage that rested on the laws of the time but even more so on Ruth.

I can think of many decisions and even friendships I entertained when God's discerning voice was loud and clear. I now realize how much silencing God's voice or that of wise counselors had the potential to delay or even cancel what God wanted to create out of my brokenness. God has a plan for the brokenhearted, and the mending process is all arranged behind the scenes by our loving Father in heaven. It will take unwavering faith in God to trust and obey every step of the way, but it is worth it. Just look at Ruth and consider how you can apply the simple principles of faith and obedience to see God do what seems impossible in your life.

Stay with God until it comes to pass.

Ruth 2:14-18

14 And at mealtime Boaz said to her, "Come here and eat some bread and dip your morsel in the wine." So she sat beside the reapers, and he passed to her roasted grain. And she ate until she was satisfied, and she had some left over.

15 When she rose to glean, Boaz instructed his young men, saying, "Let her glean even among the sheaves, and do not reproach her.

16 And also pull out some from the bundles for her and leave it for her to glean, and do not rebuke her."

17 So she gleaned in the field until evening. Then she beat out what she had gleaned, and it was about an ephah of barley.

18 And she took it up and went into the city. Her mother-in-law saw what she had gleaned. She also brought out and gave her what food she had left over after being satisfied.

Pray with me

Dear God, I do not want to do things in my own way anymore. I trust in Your perfect plan for my life. I surrender my will for Your will and my plans for your plans. In Thy name, Amen.

Finding Meaning

All praise to God, the Father of our Lord Jesus Christ. God is our merciful Father and the source of all comfort. He comforts us in all our troubles so that we can comfort others.

2 Corinthians 1:3-4a

I n search of a community, I looked for women who could relate to my new reality. I had so many deep questions and I longed for comforting answers and for validation. I needed to know how long the pain would last. I needed to know about the future; I needed an anchor; and I needed support. Unfortunately, as time went by, I found myself isolated with most of my questions left unanswered.

As a mental health professional, I am accustomed to supporting people when they are at their most vulnerable, and so it was easy for me to support a childhood friend who lost her husband and then a cousin and then a work colleague all within three years of my own loss. While I still had many questions, I also had a point of view based on my lived experience.

It was also at that time that I quietly decided in my heart that I would build that community. I have used my social media platform many times to share about my healing journey as a grieving widow, but it never dawned on me that through one viral post, I would find community and community would find me.

As I have found my own comfort in the Lord, I've taken every opportunity to point others to Him as well. Just like the story of Ruth and Naomi became a blueprint for my healing journey, I have used my own story to inspire others to find new meaning in the loss they face.

Out of my own despair, a desire was born to build hope in others. I gave pain a voice, and out of my place of grief, a purpose was born.

I believe that the hardest trials build up our faith if we are willing to be taught and grow. Through it all, I have found a special grace to carry out my calling despite what has been lost. I have truly found meaning, or perhaps it found me, when I desperately needed something to hold on to.

Pray with me

Dear God, thank you for healing my emotional wounds and for using my pain for your divine purpose. In Thy name, Amen.

Key themes: community, support, ministry

Guided Journaling:

1. Look at the key themes listed above. What key theme(s) resonate with you and why?

2. How do you define a community and what are the benefits of having one?

3. What are steps you can take to be a support to someone in your life? Write their names and what actions you can take to help them.

Extravagant Favor

So be truly glad. There is wonderful joy ahead,
even though you must endure many trials for
a little while. These trials will show that your
faith is genuine.

1 Peter 1:6-7a

The trauma I had from the loss of my husband left a bitter aftertaste.

A few months after his death, I had a dream. I was dressed in black and walking with a limp as though I had a prosthetic leg. Around the same time, my cousin happened to have a dream of me ministering to a congregation as I was wearing a prosthetic leg. One of the symbolic meanings of a prosthetic leg in a dream is that one has suffered a big injury, which was true for me.

While I was deeply affected by my broken state, I did not want the loss of my husband to define me. His loss was permanent, but this state of brokenness was meant to be temporary because my godly identity did not change despite becoming a widow. God called me to be a woman of God and His servant first and foremost. When He made me in my mother's womb, He made me alone. Therefore, from birth, I was enough on my own to see through every plan God had for me.

For a very long time, I had no joy and felt broken, but fundamentally, staying with God has been my secret weapon and my lifeline. I believe that my faith and obedience got the attention of God. According to the many promises God has for widows and orphans, God had no choice but to bless me, just as He did for Ruth and Naomi. I came to understand that God has a responsibility toward me, because He cares about me and my children and our wellbeing.

I have experienced firsthand that being part of one of the most vulnerable groups in our culture has many challenges and that I cannot afford to be distant from God. Developing a godly character that cannot be shaken by circumstance, taking heed to godly counsel and walking in obedience will continually attract God's favor. In my dryest, most broken season, God's abundant favor has been evident in my life in an extravagant way. I have learned to walk with God, in good days and bad days, and I have experienced an overflow of blessings.

Pray with me

Dear God, give me a heart to submit to your will for my life whatever trial comes my way. I trust that you see me in my distress and that there is more joy ahead. In Thy name, Amen.

Key themes: favor, obedience, purpose

Guided Journaling:

1. Look at the key themes listed above. What key theme(s) resonate with you and why?

2. Can you think of a painful life experience and how God used it to show his faithfulness to you?

3. The Bible is filled with God's promises. Find a promise that speaks to a current situation in your life, write it down and meditate on its words.

The Greatest Love Story

> *Our Father in heaven, may your name be kept*
> *holy. May your Kingdom come soon. May your*
> *will be done on earth as it is in heaven.*
>
> Matthew 6:9-10

I think about how ill-equipped I was for marriage the first time around, and I am grateful for the lived experience and all the tools I have gained in nearly two decades of life together. After my husband died, we had several signs of him which were very comforting.

Three weeks from writing this entry, I can recall crying on his shoulder in the context of a very vivid dream after going through a traumatic event. One of the most significant interactions we had after his death was in a beautiful white mansion with high ceilings and all-white decor. This was where we met face-to-face for the first time after he passed. We exchanged a few words that needed to be said. I cannot express how much closure I experienced at that moment. A heavy weight was lifted off of my shoulders; I could breathe just a little bit better.

We were perfect strangers when we met at a rest stop in Albany, NY, and for many years after, we enjoyed recalling every detail of that day. At the time, I did not know that I collided with my soul-mate, but God knew. We were engaged to be married ten months after our initial encounter, but God had to put me through the ultimate test.

Four months before our wedding day, God ordered me to pray for His blessing to move forward with our wedding which was scheduled that June. I prayed in secret for four months. Staring at my engagement ring and gazing into the eyes of our newborn, God demanded that I ask for His blessing and I did. It was the most frightening prayer one could pray, but God already knew. He simply wanted to test my faith in Him.

Our love story would last 17 years. It would be a story of ups and downs with many memorable moments I continue to cherish to this day.

Pray with me

Dear God, you are true to your promises, so I will wait confidently until my prayers are answered according to your will. In Thy name, Amen.

Key themes: prayer, wisdom, will of God

Guided Journaling:

1. Look at the key themes listed above. What key theme(s) resonate with you and why?

2. How would you describe your prayer life and how can you make it even more meaningful?

3. Reflect on an answered prayer and express your gratitude to God by writing him a *Thank You* note.

Part 3: Hope Found

A Worthy Man

And Naomi said to her daughter-in-law, "May he be blessed by the Lord, whose kindness has not forsaken the living or the dead!" Naomi also said to her, "The man is a close relative of ours, one of our redeemers."

Ruth 2:20

R uth gained favor from God and men as a result of her virtuous ways; she was a worthy woman.

Interestingly enough, the depiction of her first encounter with Boaz provides a refreshing description of what to expect from a "worthy man" (Ruth 2:1). In the second chapter of Ruth, we are introduced to a man who expresses concern, demonstrates kindness, provides resources, ensures safety and speaks blessing over the life of his future bride. In one meeting, Boaz's character is revealed.

I love the fact that this meeting was unplanned and unscripted. From the readers' perspective, both Ruth and Boaz are seen in their true light and are seemingly a good match. They are both God-fearing, kind, selfless, generous and of good moral character. The plan that God had for their union was established well before they met. Their encounter may have been unexpected in the context of their mundane lives, but it was in fact ordained by God (Ruth 2:3).

Their purpose story was written by God himself and tied to the ultimate love story of all. God has a way of using every part of our story to manifest his omnipotence and ultimately His glory. God led Ruth to Bethlehem where she would find community and ultimately find rest. Ruth needed a community to survive widowhood and meet her basic needs, but she would need Boaz to fulfill an even greater purpose (Ruth 2:9). The way she carried herself among this community made it easy for God to bless her and put her on display as a worthy woman (Ruth 3:11).

Boaz was a worthy man and a God-ordained match who complemented Ruth's godly character well. He was the man God chose to renew her joy and her hope in a brighter future. This is why we must allow God to renew our minds and restore our brokenness daily. Otherwise, we run the risk of shaping a new identity as a result of our sorrow and our emotional pain.

Ruth may have suffered a great loss, but she did not allow bitterness or sorrow to define her existence. And so, be encouraged, because on the other side of difficult life experiences, God has also prepared for you, blessings that will contribute to your healing journey.

Ruth 2:20-23

20 And Naomi said to her daughter-in-law, "May he be blessed by the Lord, whose kindness has not forsaken the living or the dead!" Naomi also said to her, "The man is a close relative of ours, one of our redeemers."

21 And Ruth the Moabite said, "Besides, he said to me, 'You shall keep close by my young men until they have finished all my harvest.'"

22 And Naomi said to Ruth, her daughter-in-law, "It is good, my daughter, that you go out with his young women, lest in another field you be assaulted."

23 So she kept close to the young women of Boaz, gleaning until the end of the barley and wheat harvests. And she lived with her mother-in-law.

Pray with me

Dear God, I pray that You would renew my mind and heal my aching heart. Increase my confidence in Your healing power and reveal Your strength in my weakness. In Thy name, Amen.

A Foreigner on God's Heart

Then Naomi, her mother-in-law said to her,
"My daughter, should I not seek rest for you,
that it may be well with you?"

Ruth 3:1

R uth was chosen to carry destiny. Her marriage to Mahlon was part of God's plan and as devastating as it was, so was his death. Their union led Ruth, born a foreigner, to the Jewish faith. We do not speak of Ruth's first husband much, but in his life and in his death, he was used to fulfill God's plan in Ruth's life. Ruth was special in the eyes of God. She was a foreigner by birth, but her life and destiny mattered more than where she was from. When she accepted to follow Naomi to Bethlehem, she expressed loyalty not only to her mother-in-law, but also to her God. She vowed, "Your people shall be my people, and your God my God. Where you die I will die, and there will I be buried. May the Lord do so to me and more also if anything but death parts me from you." (Ruth 1:16b).

When our heart turns to God, we position ourselves to partake in all of God's promise including the promise of a Savior. Indeed, the promise of a Savior was connected to a male child Ruth was destined to carry; her name is forever immortalized in the genealogy of Jesus (Ruth 4:22).

Her life circumstances did not disqualify her but rather positioned her to receive favor. God conveyed His love toward her and showed her mercy during difficult times. In those times, widows were often poor and vulnerable, and although Ruth had to suffer for a time, her story was destined to end well. The pain and suffering of loss can deter someone from their destiny for a time. It is not a sign of weakness, but rather every detour is an opportunity for God to step into our life story and change the narrative (Ruth 2:12).

Giving power to death draws in more darkness, but God's light dispels darkness and shines on the hope and glory that lies ahead. It is for each of us to find God in our dark times and seek to understand His greater plan meant to prosper us and not to harm us (Jeremiah 29:11).

Ruth 3:1-5

1 Then Naomi her mother-in-law said to her, "My daughter, should I not seek rest for you, that it may be well with you?

2 Is not Boaz our relative, with whose young women you were? See, he is winnowing barley tonight at the threshing floor.

3 Wash therefore and anoint yourself, and put on your cloak and go down to the threshing floor, but do not make yourself known to the man until he has finished eating and drinking.

4 But when he lies down, observe the place where he lies. Then go and uncover his feet and lie down, and he will tell you what to do."

5 And she replied, "All that you say I will do."

Pray with me

Dear God, give me an unwavering trust in Your plan for my life. I surrender the past I cannot change, the present and its reality, and my future, come what may. In Thy name, Amen.

Can God Trust You with Heartbreak?

He said, "And who are you?" She said, "I am Ruth, your maiden; take me under your protecting wing. You're my close relative, you know, in the circle of covenant redeemers—you do have the right to marry me."

Ruth 3:9

Haters are everywhere. They have an opinion on everything, and because their intentions are filled with dissension, there is no pleasing them.

I can only imagine what Ruth's experience was in the field. She went from gleaning in the fields among the other women to becoming the wife of Boaz, the owner of the field. My guess is that she may have had to face the court of public opinion. Some of the Hebrew women may have asked, under their breath, why God would choose a foreign woman and bless her in such a way. Why was Ruth so deserving of such a blessing?

Truth is: every woman's life is connected to a blessing that is bigger and better than what she could ever plan or execute on her own. God's will is always best, and He does not ask permission to anyone to bless us. As they say, favor is not fair and that was true for Ruth too.

She was not destined to remain alone, but she had to trust in God and trust Naomi's counsel to experience God's best. She did not allow a fear of the future to trouble her faith and delay her destiny. In fact, she acted in blind faith and did not question the process. She was focused on her part of the assignment and left the rest up to God. When the time came to redeem Ruth, Boaz need to be neither convinced nor persuaded because Ruth had executed her part flawlessly. God knew He could trust Ruth with such a challenging path.

What about you? Can God trust you with adversity? Can He get the glory out of your life as you walk through your darkest season?

Ruth followed Naomi to her country, submitted to the God of Israel and stayed in the field until her season of toil and grief was over. God blessed her for her kindness, her loyalty and her faith. Ruth's story is a beautiful depiction of suffering with grace. God was able to trust her with heartbreak. One question remains: Can God trust you with heartbreak?

Ruth 3:6-9

6 So she went down to the threshing floor and did just as her mother-in-law had commanded her.

7 And when Boaz had eaten and drunk, and his heart was merry, he went to lie down at the end of the heap of grain. Then she came softly and uncovered his feet and lay down.

8 At midnight the man was startled and turned over, and behold, a woman lay at his feet!

9 He said, "Who are you?" And she answered, "I am Ruth, your servant. Spread your wings over your servant, for you are a redeemer."

Pray with me

Dear God, I trust Your process even when my situation does not look good or feel good. I trust You because You are good. In Thy name, Amen.

Worth the Wait

For I know the plans I have for you, says the Lord. They are plans for good and not for disaster, to give you a future and a hope.

Jeremiah 29:11

E arlier this year, I experienced a desire for companionship. I had been riding solo for four years, and although I felt fulfilled in many areas of my life, I started feeling alone. I had been working from home for a few years and also attended church virtually which significantly reduced opportunities for human interaction; not to mention the pandemic. Since I also lived away from family and close friends, the feeling of isolation began to set in deeply.

Since I married at 23, the dating world was both foreign and intimidating. I timidly opened myself up only to be met with profound disappointment. That said, to be fully transparent, I would probably be married by now to a man who ended up winning my heart, but since God did not confirm this choice, I walked away from the relationship altogether.

In my walk with God, I have learned to trust His will with every detail of my life. My greatest challenge up until that point was to fully surrender my will to God and reject anything or anyone that was not sent by Him. That exercise required prayer and discernment and most importantly dying to self. Looking over my life, I took many detours as a result of my stubbornness and continue to carry many scars as a result of doing things my way. Having surrendered my healing process to God and understanding my purpose in life, I vow to marry again, only if God appoints someone to my purpose and my calling.

Since relationships are often used as a distraction by the enemy, guarding our hearts and being obedient are necessary to please God. In my first marriage, I prayed for my husband for many years before he joined the faith weeks before his untimely departure. It is a challenge to enter an interfaith or unequally yoked marriage. I have done a lot of healing work focused on relationships, love and even trauma, and at this point, I have found a true delight and peace in resting in God. It was not always the case, but when I began to discern the depth of his love for me, it changed everything.

Do not think that my goal is to appear holy or above temptation, but I have received a grace that allows me to live an unbothered life after giving my full heart to God. I am not willing to betray this kind of love with a counterfeit, temporary, partially satisfying and misaligned type of love.

Ruth was assigned to Boaz and he was God approved. Their union had a unique purpose that fulfilled their calling and ultimately glorified God.

Pray with me

Dear God, everything you have ordained for my life is worth the wait. I will guard my heart and focus on you in the waiting. In Thy name. Amen.

Key themes: dating, love of God, discernment

Guided Journaling:

1. Look at the key themes listed above. What key theme(s) resonate with you and why?

2. Have you experienced dating outside of God, how did it work out for you?

3. What are the benefits of discerning the will of God prior to taking any decision?

A Deeper Call

And we know that God causes everything to work together for the good of those who love God and are called according to his purpose for them.

Romans 8:28

Two weeks before my husband's death, I had the privilege of speaking at a woman's conference. During my prayer time leading to that day, I had one prayer: "God, introduce me to the woman you have called me to be." In other words, I knew God had called me to teach and preach, and this would be my first time operating in that gift outside of my home church.

On that day, as I stood on that podium, I was introduced to the woman God was calling to ministry. I did not consider myself qualified, but I deeply trusted the call on my life to teach the gospel.

Unbeknownst to me, this same woman called to ministry would become a widow in a few short weeks. She was the same woman with four months left to complete a three-year long ministry training program and the same one ordered to complete a 40-day fast exactly 40 days before her husband's death.

I am so glad that God calls broken people like me. Women who have tried running from God and from his truth. Women who have been called against all odds.

It was during that time that my relationship with God deepened to another level. This change was not immediate, but it would be gradual. God wanted all of me, and He finally had me in that place of full surrender.

I was once asked if I believed that God had taken my husband away, so I could fulfill God's call. While I cannot confirm or deny this assumption, I can say that God had a plan for my life that included widowhood. His way of qualifying me required total reliance and trust in Him, and this is the way it happened for me. God called me, qualified me and established me as His vessel and no one has the power to cancel my destiny – not even me. I have been on His heart and mind before I entered my mother's womb, and I accept that even what appears to be a setback is in fact part of His divine plan for my life.

Pray with me

Dear God, I often struggle when the process gets hard, but today I am reminded that you have called me to a deeper place in you. Thank you for calling broken people like me. In Thy name. Amen.

Key themes: purpose, ministry, faith

Guided Journaling:

1. Look at the Key themes listed above. What key theme(s) resonate with you and why?

2. What is God's call on your life?

3. Have you surrendered to the call God has for you or are you struggling with trusting him fully? Write about your process.

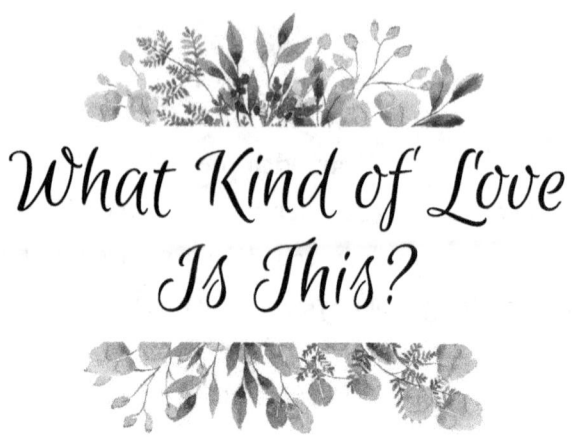

What Kind of Love Is This?

And let the peace that comes from Christ rule in your hearts.

Colossians 3:15

As a single mother of one daughter, I did not expect this kind of love to show up in my life, but it did.

A little over one month into our courtship, my late husband already knew, and he was not shy to say it out loud.

"A man who finds a wife finds a good thing and obtains favor from the Lord" (Proverbs 18:22), and while I was his good thing, he was my redeemer, saving me from the enduring shame of a painful breakup and single womanhood. In a way, he was my Boaz.

Many years later, I could look at my marriage as cut too short because of my husband's time-limited role in my life. However, instead of focusing on the void his passing has left, I allowed the love we shared and the memories we have made to overshadow his death.

As I now strive for my story of love and loss to point to God, I would like to remind you that there is only one ultimate redeemer. He loves, comforts, forgives and waits patiently until we grab a hold of the depth and breadth of His love for us. I am glad to have experienced my husband's love, but it cannot compare to the love of God.

Whether you have been loved well or whether your love story was rather bumpy, never forget that there is a love that continues to pursue you, a love that does not hurt, does not lie and does not change. The love of God is real and it is sure. He is knocking at your door today. He is hoping that you let Him in your heart again despite its broken state. He is longing for a renewed relationship with you, for an open and honest dialogue about your aching heart and deepest disappointment. God is as close as the next breath you will take.

Today is a good day to have a good cry in the arms of the Father. His kind of love is not time limited; it is eternal. A life without it would be a life devoid of life itself. He is the only one we cannot live without.

Pray with me

Dear God, heal my heart from past wounds that I've tried to hide from you and from the world and soften my heart so that I may receive your healing grace. In Thy name. Amen.

Key themes: redeemer, love, love of God

Guided Journaling:

1. Look at the key themes listed above. What key theme(s) resonate with you and why?

2. How have you experienced the unconditional love of God in your life?

3. Does your current relationship or marriage possess attributes mirroring the love of God? Give examples. If you are not in a relationship, what do you desire from a healthy relationship?

Part 4: Endless Grace

Threshing Floor

And he said, "May you be blessed by the Lord, my daughter."

Ruth 3:10a

Naomi instructed Ruth to meet Boaz at the threshing floor at nighttime. This was a risky yet calculated plan because Ruth could've been mistaken for a prostitute (Hosea 9:1) or even worse, she could've fallen prey to an evil man. She made her way to the threshing floor being very careful to hide her identity on her way to and from.

In agriculture, the threshing floor is a place where grain is separated from the chaff during harvest time. In biblical terms, the threshing floor was described as a place of separation and revelation. It was also used as a metaphor for a place where the good is separated from the bad.

As expected by Naomi, Boaz enjoyed his evening, eating and drinking before falling asleep near the pile of grain. When Boaz noticed a woman lying at his feet, he asked "Who are you?" and she answered, "I am Ruth, your servant. Spread your wings over your servant, for you are a redeemer" (Ruth 3:9).

This was Ruth's way of asking Boaz whether he would himself ask her hand in marriage, which was her heart's desire. Boaz was intentional toward Ruth and acted as a man of integrity. He took this opportunity to speak a blessing over Ruth and promised to redeem her.

While God is intentional in giving us our heart desires, we must be equally intentional in seeking wisdom and walk in integrity. As a woman who had previously experienced intimacy with a man, Ruth had to take heed to not fall into temptation. In order to be separated and set apart for God, we must resist temptation and make no excuses for living in our flesh. Leaning on our good intentions is not enough; we must lean on God who gives grace to those who fear Him and observe His commands.

Ruth and Boaz modeled integrity, self-control and fear of God and obtained God's favor according to the desire of their own hearts.

Ruth 3:10-13

10 And he said, "May you be blessed by the Lord, my daughter. You have made this last kindness greater than the first

in that you have not gone af-
ter young men, whether poor or
rich.

11 And now, my daughter, do
not fear. I will do for you all
that you ask, for all my fellow
townsmen know that you are a
worthy woman.

12 And now it is true that I
am a redeemer. Yet there is a
redeemer nearer than I.

13 Remain tonight, and in the
morning, if he will redeem you,
good; let him do it. But if he is
not willing to redeem you, then,
as the Lord lives, I will redeem
you. Lie down until the
morning."

Pray with me

Dear God, give me a divine revelation for my life and the wisdom to trade my desires for Your perfect plan. In Thy name, Amen.

Redemption Time

"Wait, my daughter, until you learn how the matter turns out, for the man will not rest but will settle the matter today."

Ruth 3:18

God has a way of positioning us for an abundant and successful life. He uses people around us and at times even strangers to bless us.

Boaz noticed Ruth in the field and inquired about her after one look. After hearing about her kindness toward Naomi and her hard work in the field, he ensured she would continue to glean in his fields. She would have access to food, water and protection, and her basic needs would be met by a man who was, still at the time, a stranger.

Ruth was moved by this unexpected benevolence which would be followed by a blessing spoken by none other than Boaz, who declared, "The Lord repay you for what you have done and a full reward be given by the Lord, the God of Israel, under whose wings you have come to take refuge" (Ruth 2:12).

Boaz made a public declaration that not only Ruth belonged to Elimelech's family, but she also belonged to the family of God. She was once a foreigner, but she would from now on benefit from the same favor as the people of the land. The story was left to be told about the blessings that God had planned for Ruth's life.

God did not forget Ruth, just like He has not forgotten about you. The detours of life may seem disheartening, but God is in control. Do not despair and stay with God, your redemption time is coming. God will remember you.

Ruth 3:14-18

14 So she lay at his feet until the morning, but arose before one could recognize another. And he said, "Let it not be known that the woman came to the threshing floor."

15 And he said, "Bring the garment you are wearing and hold it out." So she held it, and he measured out six measures

of barley and put it on her.
Then she went into the city.

16 *And when she came to her*
mother-in-law, she said, "How
did you fare, my daughter?"
Then she told her all that the
man had done for her,

17 *saying, "These six measures*
of barley he gave to me, for he
said to me, 'You must not go
back empty-handed to your m
other-in-law.'"

18 *She replied, "Wait, my*
daughter, until you learn how
the matter turns out, for the
man will not rest but will settle
the matter today."

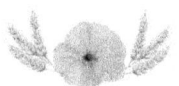

Pray with me

Dear God, I am ready for my blessing. Give me a discerning spirit and a patient heart to receive it, in your time. In Thy name, Amen.

The Dangerous Surrender

"I cannot redeem it for myself, lest I impair my own inheritance. Take my right of redemption yourself, for I cannot redeem it."

Ruth 4:6

A relationship assigned by God will always require the right time, the right life circumstance and the right person. Misalignment with any of these three steps is sure to lead to undue grief and hardship.

After meeting Boaz on the threshing floor, Ruth's life was about to change forever; her time had finally come. Her blessing was seemingly at hand (Ruth 3:11). Ruth had carefully followed Naomi's instructions. She was obedient and humble. She did everything she was expected to do. Now, only one element was missing: the right person.

In a world where instant gratification is becoming the norm, we are often pressured to take matters into our own hands. We can learn a lot from Ruth who was patient with God. Although the wait is often uncomfortable, it is also part of God's set plan. He is arranging the time, the circumstances and the actors in your story. The Scripture tells us "Let us not become weary in doing good, for at the proper time we will reap a harvest if we do not give up" (Galatians 6:9).

Ruth never gave up and believed in a better tomorrow. She acted in faith when she bathed and put on perfume. She acted in faith when she laid at Boaz's feet. She acted in great faith when she announced to Boaz that he was one of her family's kinsman redeemers. And while Boaz let her know that he was not the closest relative to fulfill this duty, Ruth was not dissuaded. She returned home in the morning and waited with Naomi until the matter was settled.

Surrender requires trust and total abandonment and this was a dangerous surrender because Ruth put everything on the line and her fate was now in Boaz's hands. God prepares the hearts of those who are meant to bless us and Boaz's heart was postured to fulfill this duty. God changes times and seasons, as it is written in Daniel 2:21, and He did so for Ruth. She surrendered fully and God blessed her exceedingly, abundantly, above all she could ask or think (Ephesians 3:20).

Ruth 4:1-6

1 Now Boaz had gone up to the

gate and sat down there. And behold, the redeemer, of whom Boaz had spoken, came by. So Boaz said, "Turn aside, friend; sit down here." And he turned aside and sat down.

2 And he took ten men of the elders of the city and said, "Sit down here." So they sat down.

3 Then he said to the redeemer, "Naomi, who has come back from the country of Moab, is selling the parcel of land that belonged to our relative Elimelech.

4 So I thought I would tell you of it and say, 'Buy it in the presence of those sitting here and in the presence of the elders of my people.' If you will redeem it, redeem it. But if you will not, tell me, that I may know, for there is no one besides you to redeem it, and I come after you." And he said, "I will re-

deem it."

5 Then Boaz said, "The day you buy the field from the hand of Naomi, you also acquire Ruth the Moabite, the widow of the dead, in order to perpetuate the name of the dead in his inheritance."

6 Then the redeemer said, "I cannot redeem it for myself, lest I impair my own inheritance. Take my right of redemption yourself, for I cannot redeem it."

Pray with me

Dear God, in the midst of the chaos I know that you are in control. I surrender my will to you and give you thanks for working everything out for my good. In Thy name, Amen.

Self-Compassion

I will comfort those who mourn, bringing words of praise to their lips. May they have abundant peace, both near and far, says the Lord who heals them.

Isaiah 57:18b-19

Sometimes, we blame our unfortunate circumstances on God, when in fact many of the challenges we face are natural consequences of our own life choices. We self-sabotage and compromise the opportunities we are given and often lack self-accountability.

Looking back on my healing journey, I wish I could do many things differently. Some decisions and friendships I rushed into left me aggravated and scared. I have found that constantly asking God for wisdom and moving slowly has led me to better outcomes.

In October 2020, I sold my house 19 months after my husband's passing and moved back home to Canada and be closer to my family of origin. Since my husband died in our house, it was very traumatic to walk past our living room for a long time, let alone sit in it. I will never forget the day after his death, the temperature of the entire main level of the house was freezing cold. It was unreal and I had to call my children to ask if they felt it too. I still miss that house, because it was an answered prayer and a dream come true, and sometimes, I wonder if I had made the right move by leaving so hurriedly.

In friendships and relationships, I earned extra scars from not discerning the heart of people who were attaching themselves to me. I have forgiven myself because I know now that I was vulnerable and operating from my trauma experience. For four years, I buried myself in my work and climbed the corporate ladder at the expense of my fragile heart and mind. I compromised my healing and my wellbeing and had to be intentional about finding tools and resources to jumpstart my healing journey.

One of my biggest regrets is not welcoming God in every aspect of my healing journey, while one of my biggest lessons has been to learn and adopt self-compassion as a tool to forgive myself and turn kindness inwardly. In this season of my life, I am strongly committed to show up for you and everyone assigned to my voice and my calling. I want to share my story of love and loss and help women facing painful experiences grow in their faith. The more detours we take on this healing journey, the more setbacks and traps for the enemy to use against you and me. We are called to be unwavering in our faith and teach the lessons we have learned. We do not get to make excuses, but we can learn and grow together.

Pray with me

Dear God, I receive your forgiveness and I forgive myself for the mistakes of the past. In Thy name. Amen.

Key themes: accountability, vulnerability, healing journey

Guided Journaling:

1. What key theme(s) resonate with you? Select one or more themes and journal your thoughts.

2. Think of a situation you blamed God for instead of taking personal responsibility. What lessons did you learn?

3. What are some practical steps you can take in beginning or furthering your healing journey?

Carried by Grace

You allowed me to suffer much hardship, but
you will restore me to life again and lift me up
from the depths of the earth.

Psalm 71:20

Sometimes, I wish I was not so well acquainted with hardship, but then again, I would not be so well acquainted with God. I love Ruth's story, because it depicts the timing and sovereignty of God in a way that acknowledges both the hard times while magnifying the goodness of God.

When my husband died, I entered a season of physical, emotional, mental and spiritual battle. I lost so much weight overnight, experienced panic attacks, dragged myself out of bed to pray on the living room floor every morning before driving 1.5 hrs to work each way to maintain a roof over my family's head.

I was on autopilot, and I was exhausted. I did not cry much for a very long time. I mindlessly went about each day, like the previous one: No hope, no expectations, no vision for my future, just a deep feeling of emptiness and loss.

I do not even remember what my prayers were about, but I am so grateful that God had called me to a fast, prior to this dark season, because I would need to make several withdrawals from that prayer bank for months to come. Restoration was gradual for me. It was not overnight, and while I am in a much better place, the shadow of the loss remains. It just does not have a hold on me anymore.

Every season has a beginning and an endpoint, and I now realize that as long as I held on ever so tightly to the darkness, I was not making room for the light to come in. As long as fear overwhelmed my thoughts, there was no room for faith to abide. While God desired to give me a garment of praise for the weight of heaviness, He would not force it on me. Instead, I would have to give Him permission to heal me in and out of season and allow the weight of His glory to overwhelm me. In the midst of that season, it was grace that carried me. The prayers of faithful prayer warriors held me up and covered me; I could literally feel grace hovering all around me. The progress I have made started with my choice and desire to heal from deep grief. The rest has been all God.

Pray with me

Dear God, although I cannot see it or feel it, I rest in the knowing that my healing is on its way. You desire that I be made whole and I believe that it is so. In Thy name. Amen.

Key themes: favor, obedience, grace

Guided Journaling:

1. What key theme(s) resonate with you? Select one or more themes and journal your thoughts.

2. Describe a time God's grace carried you through a difficult time?

3. They say that *Trouble don't last always*. Looking back over your life, how do you relate to that saying?

Where Is Home Now?

And Jesus said to the woman, "Your faith has saved you; go in peace."

Luke 7:50

While life is unpredictable, nothing takes God by surprise. One of the greatest lessons I've learned in my healing journey is that God did not promise me my plans, but rather His plan to prosper me and not to harm me, to give me a hope and a future (Jeremiah 29:11). I have always been very goal oriented. I was a master at planning my life, setting goals and executing my plans. I describe my adult life as a castle of cards. Over two decades, I built my castle thoughtfully and carefully, and just when I was finally getting to my definition of success, the whole thing came tumbling down.

It took me four years to "see" myself again in the future. I could not think about the future, because I could not fathom a different life than the one I planned. I sold our family home, which was supposed to be the homebase our grandchildren would visit, and where my husband would cook all of our favorite meals for years to come. I grieved not only him, but what life used to be or would've been. I grieved the trips we never took because of our busy lives and raising a young family. I grieved about our family holiday traditions. I even grieved never getting to shop for our two patio chairs which were meant for our new deck: one for him and one for me.

This journal entry is not about a castle of cards or the patio chairs. Instead, it is about the plan of God for our life and where the journey will take us. It takes a whole lot of faith to keep going after facing any type of loss or difficult life transition, but I promise you that you are never alone on the journey. To God, there are no surprises, and as long as you keep Him in the narrative, you will see the imprints of His sovereignty in your own life, because He is always in control. He did it for Ruth and Naomi; He is doing it for me, and I have faith that He will work it out for you as well.

Pray with me

Dear God, I place my faith and my future in your hands. I surrender my will and give you permission to take control of my life. Lead and I will follow. In Thy name. Amen.

Key themes: loss, faith, future

Guided Journaling:
1. What key theme(s) resonate with you? Select one or more themes and journal your thoughts.

2. Loss is experienced in many ways. Write about a loss that has been particularly difficult for you to process (examples include loved ones, job loss, separation, divorce, etc)?

3. How did this situation impact your faith in God?

Part 5: Building the House

Joy Is Here

"We are witnesses. May the Lord make the woman, who is coming into your house, like Rachel and Leah, who together built up the house of Israel."

Ruth 4:11a

Naomi had left Judah as a married woman with two sons only to return empty. Upon her return, the women inquired about her and Naomi said to them, "Do not call me Naomi; call me Mara for the Almighty has dealt very bitterly with me, I went away full, and the Lord brought me back empty (Ruth 1:20-21).

She must have dreaded facing her community. The thought of answering insensitive questions just to satisfy the curiosity of old friends must have been an unnerving experience. Naomi thought the Lord had turned His back on her after losing her husband, her sons, her social status, her security, but most importantly God's favor.

When we face significant misfortune and hardship, it is easy to let discouragement change our perception of life, of our identity and even our perception of God. While Naomi called herself Mara, which means bitter, God had a plan to restore her joy. While death is final and permanent, the attributes of God are also permanent and do not change. He is indeed El Shaddai–God Almighty–and there is nothing he cannot do. Naomi would smile again from a deep place. God had a plan that would give new meaning to her life.

After Ruth gave birth to a son, the women she had met upon her return blessed the Lord for Naomi's redeemer and testified "the Lord shall be to you a restorer of life and nourisher of your old age" (Ruth 4: 15). Naomi's beauty for ashes (Isaiah 61:3) would be manifested in the birth of Obed (Ruth 4:13), who would become King David's grandfather (Ruth 4:22).

Naomi's life purpose was redefined as she would watchover the newborn as his nurse. God remembered Naomi as He will also remember you.

Ruth 4:7-13

7 Now this was the custom in former times in Israel concerning redeeming and exchanging: to confirm a transaction, the one drew off his sandal and gave it to the other, and this was the manner of attesting in Israel.

8 So when the redeemer said to Boaz, "Buy it for yourself," he drew off his sandal.

9 Then Boaz said to the elders and all the people, "You are witnesses this day that I have bought from the hand of Naomi all that belonged to Elimelech and all that belonged to Chilion and to Mahlon.

10 Also Ruth the Moabite, the widow of Mahlon, I have bought to be my wife, to perpetuate the name of the dead in his inheritance, that the name of the dead may not be cut off from among his brothers and from the gate of his native place. You are witnesses this day."

11 Then all the people who were at the gate and the elders said, "We are witnesses. May the Lord make the woman, who is coming into your house, like Rachel and Leah, who together built up the house of Israel. May you act worthily in Ephrathah and be renowned in Bethlehem,

12 and may your house be like the house of Perez, whom Tamar bore to Judah, because of the offspring that the Lord will give you by this young woman."

13 So Boaz took Ruth, and she became his wife. And he went into her, and the Lord gave her conception, and she bore a son.

Pray with me

Dear God, thank You for defining my purpose and for hiding my identity in You and not in what I go through. Renew my joy daily so I can tell of Your goodness and faithfulness. In Thy name, Amen.

Casting Our Crowns

"Blessed be the Lord, who has not left you this day without a redeemer, and may his name be renowned in Israel!"

Ruth 4:14

It would've been understandable for Naomi and Ruth to make their mourning and grief an idol. Afterall, they had suffered much loss and trauma in a short period of time. While they had to process the grief, God would not allow them to be stuck in that grief.

Shifting perspective from the past to the future requires a change of mindset and perhaps for some, a change of environment. Naomi and Ruth had to leave Moab, where their past lived because God was calling them away from death to where he had visited his people (Ruth 1: 6). Ruth demonstrated great faith when she left her home and her pagan gods and joined the Jewish faith. Even when Naomi called herself Mara, as she felt afflicted by God, she expressed her bitter disposition, but did not lose her faith.

It is difficult to walk through a healing journey when we have to face difficult circumstances and not lose our faith. As believers, we are instructed to pick up our cross, figuratively, and follow Christ. For Ruth and Naomi, that cross was heavy and showed no mercy, but I am so glad that the cross also means victory. Denying ourselves for the cause of Christ is an expectation of our faith walk. In doing so, we are blessed and receive favor from God. Ruth and Naomi pressed forward and were rewarded with a bright future. Boaz married Ruth and was blessed with a son, Obed. Ruth prioritized the comfort and care of her mother-in-law and was rewarded for her kindness. Naomi was able to preserve her late husband's inheritance and was also comforted with the birth of Obed.

God is willing and able to provide for all of our needs, but we have to do our part in prioritizing His will and His godly standards. Our willingness to humble ourselves and make Him sovereign Lord over our life is sure to lead us to a favorable future.

Ruth 4:14-17

14 Then the women said to Naomi, "Blessed be the Lord, who has not left you this day without a redeemer, and may his name be renowned in Israel!

*15 He shall be to you a restor-
er of life and a nourisher of
your old age, for your daughter-in-law who loves you, who is
more to you than seven sons, has
given birth to him."*

*16 Then Naomi took the child
and laid him on her lap and
became his nurse.*

*17 And the women of the
neighborhood gave him a
name, saying, "A son has been
born to Naomi." They named
him Obed. He was the father of
Jesse, the father of David.*

Pray with me

Dear God, change my mourning into a bountiful praise. Fill my
heart with glorious joy and perfect peace. In Thy name, Amen.

God's Divine Will

Your kingdom come, your will be done, on earth as it is in heaven.

Matthew 6:10

Imagine losing your spouse and then leaving your home just to find yourself in a different country, a foreign culture and a new faith. While we are not told explicitly how Ruth coped with pain, we can assume that she mourned and grieved her many losses while also adapting to her new life.

They say that healing is a movement and in that process, we hold on to some things and some things we must let go of. In Ruth's case, she seemed to have put her personal interests and needs aside and focused solely on taking care of her mother-in-law by taking on the responsibility of providing for their household. Little did she know that God's divine will would lead her to building a family of her own in the near future.

Only God sees the full picture of our life and for that reason, we can learn through Ruth's story to not question his will. If God holds the world in his hands, we should also trust that He sees each of us and commands our destiny. We can rest assured that He has our best interest at the center of His promises and wait patiently for the revealing of His will.

Our calling is often revealed through adversity and every confusing and frustrating step is a part of His plan. Sometimes the wait seems long as God develops our character in order to prepare us for our blessing. If we are willing to submit to the process and not shy away from painful experiences, we can also be used by God. Some of us must learn humility, while others work on cultivating patience and building up our faith.

Ultimately, God used a poor widowed foreigner to build the house of Israel which was not only an unexpected plot twist but also a demonstration of God's goodness and kindness. At the very end of the Book of Ruth, it is written that Obed fathered Jesse, and Jesse fathered David (Ruth 4:22). Prophecy had to be fulfilled and Ruth the Moabite was interwoven with the building of the house of Israel.

Ruth 4:18-22

18 Now these are the generations of Perez: Perez fathered Hezron,

19 *Hezron fathered Ram, Ram fathered Amminadab,*

20 *Amminadab fathered Nahshon, Nahshon fathered Salmon,*

21 *Salmon fathered Boaz, Boaz fathered Obed,*

22 *Obed fathered Jesse, and Jesse fathered David.*

Pray with me

Dear God, give me faith to believe in Your plan for my life and patiently wait on You no matter how long the testing of my faith may take. In Thy name, Amen.

Dependable God

For you know that when your faith is tested,
your endurance has a chance to grow.

James 1:3

Just like each Winter must honor the course of nature and make room for Spring, my deep sorrow eventually made room for a fresh perspective on life and a renewed purpose. The death of my husband marked the end of a chapter of my life that I did not expect to close so soon. To be perfectly honest, prior to his passing, I took the comforts of marriage and our financial security for granted. I was self-reliant in many ways and obsessively planned every aspect of my life, never suspecting that my control issues would be tested well beyond me.

Self-reliance is a dangerous trap because it leaves no room for God to operate in a sovereign way. It also feeds a spirit of pride, leaving God as an option instead of the principle authority. Truth is, life happens and we must learn to ride the waves. The storms of life are opportunities for God to operate miracles in our lives.

Two hours before writing this entry, my employer shared some unfortunate updates about the business, which would significantly impact my yearly wages in as little as 15 days. I had never been in this position before and was totally blindsided. All the self-reliance in the world could not help me. I've had to depend on God before and this was another test. I was shaken, but I did not allow panic to set in. God had been faithful again and again and again, so why not trust Him once more.

Some may wonder why a good God allowed this to happen? While I do not hold the answer to this question, I have assurance that I've never seen the righteous forsaken nor his seed begging bread (Psalm 37:25). God is looking for a Ruth-like faith. A faith that does not question the goodness of God when facing difficulties. A faith that believes that "all things work together for good for those who love God" (Romans 8:28a). The imprints of God's sovereignty have left an indelible mark in every chapter of my life story. God is building a monument of faith with my life while I rest on his promises despite the storm.

Pray with me

Dear God, your spoken word changes everything. Say a word in my favor and silence the voice of those who wish me harm. In Thy name. Amen.

Key themes: pride, adversity, faith

Guided Journaling:

1. What key theme(s) resonate with you? Select one or more themes and journal your thoughts.

2. What area of your life or decision can you surrender to God in this season of your life?

3. Write a prayer of faith for what you are believing God to do as it relates to your previous answer.

God of All Grace

Praise the Lord; praise God our savior! For each day he carries us in his arms. Our God is a God who saves! The Sovereign Lord rescues us from death.

Psalm 68:19

I have been asked far too many times whether I considered dating and marrying again. The truth is, I have considered marriage, but dating in your forties is a scary proposition. See, this was not part of my life plan. I did not plan on sleeping in my bed alone as I neared my forties, nor did I expect my sweet labradoodle to sleep in my bed every night, as if he knew that the old rule of no laying on mom's bed was a thing of the past. I certainly did not plan to parent four teenage girls alone and figure out how to be strong for each of them. But God is a keeper and He has kept us.

I have had to trust God with every detail of my life, and depend on His guidance and wisdom. I made good choices and some poor choices, but God has given me grace. It was very daunting to carry the weight of all household responsibilities on my shoulders. We could no longer play "good cop, back cop" in raising our children. I was "IT" all of the time and was left alone to figure it all out.

I am so thankful that God is the "defender of widows" (Psalm 68:5) and has intended many promises for widows and orphans. And what a relief it was for me to discover so many of them. Ultimately, losing my spouse left more room for God, but frankly, this is by choice. Once I made peace with God's will, I availed myself to discover Him in a fresh and new dimension. There was more room, more time, more intention to know Him, serve Him and please Him. I understand more and more that my life is less about my marriage or even my children who are getting older and will eventually leave the nest. God is giving me grace to overcome life's difficulties, so I can instill hope in those who will need my story and my voice to overcome their own adversities.

I believe that we are all called to be living epistles and that in the end, each of our stories should ultimately point to God.

Pray with me

Dear God, thank you for a renewed mind and a fresh perspective on what really matters in life. In Thy name. Amen.

Key themes: parenting, ministry, grace

Guided Journaling:

1. What key theme(s) resonate with you? Select one or more themes and journal your thoughts.

2. Is God asking you to make more room for him? What activities or habits are you willing to trade off to spend more time in God's presence?

3. How does your life point to God? Give some concrete examples.

Building God's Kingdom at All Cost

He will wipe every tear from their eyes, and
there will be no more death or sorrow or crying
or pain. All these things are gone forever.

Revelation 21:4

W e each have a cross to bear and do not get to decide our fate in that way (Luke 14:27). We only have control over the way we navigate the challenges that we face everyday.

In order to gracefully walk through losing my spouse, I needed a measure of faith that stretched me like never before, and although some days are still hard, I know that my strength is deeply related to my faith and my belief in God. It would've been easy to fall into a victim role, but no one would benefit or grow from my experience if I had chosen to wallow in my grief. I had to come to a place where I stopped asking "why me" and traded this question for "why not". It was also then that I knew that God intentionally chose me. He knew exactly the woman I would be on the other side of the loss. I am now in a place where my relationship with God is the one that matters most over any other relationship. More trusting and no longer wavering; more believing and less questioning. I can never be too attached to a person and give their life or death more importance than God himself.

The Scripture says, "If you come to me but will not leave your family, you cannot be my follower. You must love me more than your father, mother, wife, children, brothers, and sisters—even more than your own life! Whoever will not carry the cross that is given to them when they follow me cannot be my follower" (Luke 14:26-27).

My faith has grown, as I trusted the God who chose me and marked my life with a destiny far greater than the loss, the pain and the grief I faced. I no longer limit my worldview to what my eyes can see and what my mind can comprehend, because I have seen God do what I thought was impossible. I cannot afford to idolize death when God has called me to build His kingdom on earth that we may inherit eternal life. God chose women like you and I to show the world how to walk gracefully through adversity and how to depend on Him for healing. The world needs the healed version of us; destiny awaits.

Pray with me

Dear God, thank you for using my story of love, loss and healing to gain a deeper faith in you. Thank you for choosing my story and for turning it into a testimony. In Thy name. Amen.

Key themes: faith, kingdom of God, destiny

Guided Journaling:

1. What key theme(s) resonate with you? Select one or more themes and journal your thoughts.

2. What concrete actions can you take to inspire other women with your life story?

3. What is the evidence of your commitment to building the kingdom of God?

About the author

Dr. Mia McNeil is a clinical leader, minister, educator, and a voice of comfort in the realm of grief and healing. Founder of the Hello Healing Network, she dedicates her work to helping others transform their pain into pathways for personal growth and resilience. Drawing on her own experiences and professional expertise, Dr. McNeil advocates for a journey of healing that can unlock profound transformation and enhance life quality. Residing in Eastern Pennsylvania, she is a devoted mother to four daughters and finds joy in reading, writing, and traveling. With "Chosen," she makes her heartfelt debut as an author, offering guidance to those navigating loss and seeking renewal.

Find out more about her work at
https://www.McneilPsychiatric.com.

Acknowledgements

I would like to express my deepest gratitude to all those who have supported and encouraged me throughout this journey of writing this book. Your unwavering belief in me has been my guiding light, and I am truly grateful for each one of you.

To my daughters Tammy, Ryan, Alexis and Emily, for their endless love, understanding, and patience during the long hours I spent immersed in this project. Your support means everything to me, and I am so fortunate to have you by my side. To my grandson Malcolm, you have stolen my heart and are my gift from God. To my parents, Smith and Margareth, my sister Danoe, my brother Luc-Edouard and my sister-in-love Micherose and to my entire village, I am grateful for your unwavering support. A special mention to Kathleen, thank you for holding space for me consistently for the past 5 years.

To my friends Tracy, Rachelle and Magalie, who cheered me on, offered words of encouragement, listened to my ideas with enthusiasm and prayed for me consistently and for the success of this book. Your friendship has been a source of strength and inspiration for my own spiritual journey, and I am grateful for your presence in my life. To the most supportive project manager Esther, thank you for your wisdom, hard work and prayers. Your walk with the Lord inspires me. To my girlfriends Leslie, Elizabeth, MaryAnn and Anjie, thank you for your friendship through the years and especially during my darkest season. Our friendship has stood the test of distance and time. You never stopped believing in me.

I want to extend my heartfelt thanks to my beta readers. Throughout the beta reading process, you were not only diligent readers but also a trusted advisor. Your feedback was comprehensive, thoughtful, and constructive. You took the time to delve into the story, characters, and themes, providing me with a fresh perspective that greatly enhanced the overall quality of the book.

I am deeply indebted to the editors at Beverly House Press, whose keen insights, sharp eye for detail, and unwavering dedication have transformed this manuscript into a work that I am truly proud of. Your expertise has been invaluable, and I am so grateful for the opportunity to work with you. A special thanks to the book cover designer for delivering a quality product.

I would also like to thank Dr. Tiffanie Yael Maoz for your leading role and the team at Beverly House Press, for their hard work, professionalism, and support throughout the publishing process. Your commitment to excellence has made this journey a truly rewarding one. I am grateful for Dr. Barbara Schwarck for connecting us and for guiding me during a pivotal period of my life. Your skillful and compassionate interventions led me to deeper healing and emotional breakthroughs that have transformed my personal and professional life forever.

Last but certainly not least, I want to express my appreciation to the readers of this book. Your curiosity, open-mindedness, and passion for healing and growing in faith inspire me to continue writing and sharing stories with the world. Thank you for giving my words a chance to resonate with you.

To all those mentioned here and to those whose names I may have inadvertently left out, please know that your contributions have not gone unnoticed. This book would not have been possible without your support, and for that, I am truly grateful.

Get Your Free Grief Guide

Are you looking for guidance and support on your journey through grief?

My e-book offers compassionate insights, practical strategies, and heartfelt stories to help you navigate the challenges of loss. Discover ways to embrace healing, find meaning and honor your loved ones as you move forward!

Let's walk this journey together. Let's heal together!

https://www.McneilPsychiatric.com/free-grief-guide

www.ingramcontent.com/pod-product-compliance
Lightning Source LLC
Chambersburg PA
CBHW071516120626
46550CB00006B/2241